Flowing with Seasons

Art Aeon

Art Aeon/*Flowing with Seasons* [2nd Edition]

ISBN: 9781990060045

Publisher: AEON PRESS, Halifax, Nova Scotia, Canada
E-mail: canaeonpress@gmail.com

Copyright holder: ART AEON WORKS LLC

All rights reserved. No part of this publication may be reproduced, stored in a retrieval system, or transmitted, in any form or by any means without the prior written permission of artaeon@artaeonworks.com.

An old version of this book was published in 2003 by AEON PRESS under the title:
Flowing with Seasons [1st Edition] by Art Aeon.

<Revised: March 2025>

Books of Poetry by Art Aeon

Flowing with Seasons (2003)
Hymn to Shining Mountains: The Canadian Rockies (2004)
In the Range of Light: The Yosemite (2005)
Snowflakes on Old Pines (2006)
Prayer to Sea (2007)
Echoes from Times Past (2008)
Breathing in Dao [道] (2009)
The Final Day of Socrates (2010)
Beyond the Tragedies of Oedipus and Antigone (2011)
Dù Fǔ [杜 甫] *and a Pilgrim* (2012)
The Yosemite: Images and Echoes (2013)
Revealing Dream of Vergil (2014)
Homer and Odysseus (2017)
Socrates with Xantippe on his Last Day (2019)*
Tragic Comedies of Humans (2019)*
Du Fu [杜 甫] *with his Last Pilgrim* (2019)*
Virgil's Last Dream of Aeneas and Homer (2019)*
Following Homer's Odyssey (2020)*
Human Causes of the Trojan War (2020)*
Awakening to One's Conscience (2020)*
Dante's Sublime Poem of Light (2022)*
On the Nature of Humankind (2022)*
Cosmic Drama of Nature (2022)*
Tribute to Mentors and Friends (2023)*
Pilgrimage into Classics (2024)*
Simple Songs on Life in Nature (2024)*
***Inner Voice**{2000-2007}: Simple Songs on Nature*(2024)*

*Distributed worldwide by Amazon.com as printed books
and by Google Play Books.com as electronic books.

Flowing with Seasons

For

whoever toils in earnest
to fulfil the journey of our life
with devotion, fortitude, and love.

List of Poems

	{1}	*Family Hiking*
First Cycle	{2}	*Rainbow*
of Seasons	{3}	*Bay at Dusk*
	{4}	*Our Children at Play*
	{5}	*In Rain*
Second Cycle	{6}	*Free at Sea*
of Seasons	{7}	*Autumn Elegy*
	{8}	*Walking Home on Snow*
	{9}	*Shy Spring*
Third Cycle	{10}	*Summer Dream*
of Seasons	{11}	*Painting Autumn*
	{12}	*Blizzard*
	{13}	*Calm Sea*
Fourth Cycle	{14}	*Summer Repose*
of Seasons	{15}	*Autumn Moon*
	{16}	*Winter Blues*

List of Poems

	{17}	*Spring Prayer*
5th Cycle	{18}	*Daydreaming at Sea*
	{19}	*Autumn Leaves*
	{20}	*Snowy Night*
	{21}	*Languid Spring*
6th Cycle	{22}	*Praying on a Canoe*
	{23}	*Inner Autumn*
	{24}	*Winter Journey*
	{25}	*Spring Stroll*
7th Cycle	{26}	*Birds' Footprints*
	{27}	*Autumn Night*
	{28}	*Snowy Village*
	{29}	*Spring Storm*
8th Cycle	{30}	*Summer Sunset*
	{31}	*Rumination*
	{32}	*Mute Songs*

List of Poems

	{33}	*Wandering Carefree*
9th Cycle	{34}	*Dews on a Rose*
	{35}	*Migrating Birds*
	{36}	*On Freezing Seashores*
	{37}	*Dismal Spring*
10th Cycle	{38}	*Evening Stroll*
	{39}	*Autumn Woods*
	{40}	*Seasons' Flow*
	{41}	*For Roses and Poems*
11th Cycle	{42}	*Gardening*
	{43}	*Touch of Autumn*
	{44}	*Winter Desolation*
	{45}	*Uneasy Spring*
12th Cycle	{46}	*Dawn*
	{47}	*Autumn Rose*
	{48}	*Footprints on Snow*

List of Poems

13th Cycle	{49}	*Spring Mists*
	{50}	*Daydreaming*
	{51}	*Moonlit Garden*
	{52}	*Tides*
14th Cycle	{53}	*Chilly Spring*
	{54}	*Blessing*
	{55}	*Toil and Prayer*
	{56}	*A Wanderer*
15th Cycle	{57}	*Ode to Spring*
	{58}	*A Heron*
	{59}	*Eloquent Autumn*
	{60}	*In a Waking Dream?*

{1}

Family Hiking

In a pleasant, cheerful new spring,
we hike along pristine seacoasts.

The sun is so bright and warm.
The air tastes so fresh and sweet.

The sky soars up high and clear.
The sea extends vast and deep.

Humming plain hymns to ourselves,
we exalt nature in awe with love.

Rainbow

A graceful rainbow
dips into the sea
over the horizon
at a calm sunset.

How ethereal and
mysterious it looks
like an enchanting dream,
painted aloft in the sky.

A lone wayfarer kneels
to pray in heartfelt thanks
for the sublime beauty
of nature in a trance.

The Bay at Dusk

After a long day's work,
I stop by the serene bay.
Clouds wreathe the setting sun
with pale, vague haloes.

   The calm water reflects
   subtle lights and shades.
   A seagull hovers over
   colourful autumn seashores.

   Gentle dusk deepens
   in tranquillity.
   A lone shade of man
   bows in solitude.

Our Children at Play

On a bright, sunny winter day,
we hike through forests in deep snow.
A small frozen lake invites us
to enjoy its wondrous playground.

What fun it is to slide on the ice!
Our children's shouts of sheer delight
echo through the woods and my heart.
Beautiful is the young at heart.

In Rain

Spring showers quench
bare, dry ground's thirsts.
Beneath dead leaves,
new green buds sprout.

Thin mists embrace
vibrant seashores.
Soaking in spring rain,
a meek man sits still.

Free at Sea

A sleek kayak
glides on the sea.

Cool, playful waves
splash on my face.

Refreshing breezes
caress my body.

I feel so happy
carefree on water.

Autumn Elegy

Bleak, chilly rains fall
on sad, fallen leaves.
Dark clouds suffocate
the livid land and sea.

Passionate yearnings
in sober loneliness—
Yet, how deeply I care
these sombre autumn days.

Walking Home on Snow

In serene dusk, I walk home alone
after a fulfilling day's work.
The crescent moon smiles in the sky,
filled with beautiful twinkling stars.

I hop and hum like a little child,
gladly walking home on a sea of fresh snow:
To reach the warm hearth at our sweet home
where my beloved family waits for me.

Shy Spring

Long, cold, severe
winter retreats.
Slow, shy, timid
spring comes at last.
Its gentle breath
cheers up our hearts.

Nature gently flows
in mystical rhythms.
It holds us in awe
with breathtaking suspense.
Then, it inspires us
with vital actions.

Summer Dream

Fine summer days flow
like beautiful dreams.

Exquisite roses exude
fresh, wondrous fragrances.

Hard work invigorates
our soul as well as our body.

May heartfelt poems grow
from my tears, sweat, and blood.

Painting Autumn

Like an artist
inspired with insight,
I strive to paint
into my memory
vibrant sublime lights
and subtle shades
of this deep, colourful,
pensive autumn,
with colourless,
plain words in awe.

Blizzard

A blinding snowstorm
ravages this bleak land.
Fierce, freezing gales gust
through rugged seacoasts.

The enraged sea roars,
hidden in thick fogs.
Powerful waves pound
frozen, craggy cliffs.

A man watches the storm
on a bare, stark headland,
trembling at its austere
yet breathtaking beauty.

Calm Spring Sea

Picturesque white clouds
sail aloft in the blue sky.

The vast sea reposes
in an unearthly calm.

The curved horizon afar
merges with the beyond.

A humble reed bows
in gentle spring breezes.

Summer Repose

To rest after hard work,
I listen to blissful music.

Balmy breezes gently embrace
my shadow cast on calm water.

The sun sets quietly.
Serenity deepens in my heart.

Autumn Moon

The bright, full moon rises
above tranquil seashores.

A lone bird flies away
over the gleaming sea.

The autumn deepens
in colourful leaves.

Gentle solitude
consoles a meek soul.

Winter Blues

Dark, sombre dusk shrouds
gloomy, dank, dismal streets.

Bleak shadows hurry
in uneasy confusion.

Severe blizzards freeze
sad, listless, numb hearts.

A desolate soul wafts
in a dream of spring.

Spring Prayer

Balmy breaths of the shy, new spring
gently pervade my humble heart.

New buds sprout beneath bare soils
to bloom into graceful flowers.

Cheerful tunes of cute larks awake me
from the long, languid winter's sleep.

I scribble mute words on blank pages,
praying that they may bloom into pure songs.

{18}

Daydreaming at Sea

Subtle, delicate mists veil
mystic, pristine seacoasts.

A shade of man muses
adrift on a lone canoe:

"Why do you dream of reaching
the unknown shore? It is too hard
for an ephemeral man.
This dream is too abstruse
for you to grasp its meaning."

Autumn Leaves

Ripe, deep autumn paints
tall, majestic trees
with brilliant hues:
Red, brown, and yellow.

A meek man collects
vivid fallen leaves.
He reads wordless verses
engraved on each leaf.

{20}

Snowy Night

Soft snow gently falls
in a silent night.
Pure, white flowers bloom
amid this dead, cold winter.

Stately trees exult
in stoic delights.
This bleak, stark world changes
into a beauteous dreamland.

Dozing by a warm hearth,
a humble man dreams
of vivid, eternal blooms
of graceful flowers in his heart.

Languid Spring

Days after dull, chilly days,
it drizzles endlessly.

Heavy, low clouds shroud
this gloomy, lethargic land.

The inert sea looks
like a livid bog.

My torpid mind drowses
in vague, languid dreams.

Praying on a Canoe

Gentle afterglows
of the serene sunset
imbue the pristine seashores
with subtle lights and shades.

The tranquil bay looks like
a huge crystal mirror.
A lone canoe glides on
the calm, limpid water.

Everything reposes
in ethereal peace.
A humble man bows
to the sublime beauty in bliss.

Inner Autumn

Colourful autumn leaves
gently fall off from trees.

They weave on the blank ground
vivid, abstruse patterns.

How gracefully Mother
Nature bedecks herself!

Yet, who would dream up
this inner autumn,
deepening in my mind?

Winter Journey

Gloomy, heavy clouds hover over
this desolate, bleak land.

Bare trees bravely bear up
blinding, severe blizzards.

A lone wanderer keeps on
the journey to his dreamland.

Spring Stroll

A brief afterglow
of the sunset fades away.

A wondrous cloud floats
in the serene spring sky.

Subtle dusk pervades
calm, misty, dreamy seashores.

A pensive man strolls
in deep solitude.

Birds' Footprints

On a quiet sandy beach at sunset,
little birds leave tiny footprints.

Suffused with gentle afterglows,
playful waves caress them.

How cryptic yet wondrous they look
like mystic poems from a fairyland!

Autumn Night

On a crisp, serene autumn night,
suffused by bright, lucent moonlight,
I alone stay awake in solemn solitude.

Fallen leaves cover the bleak ground.
Nothing stirs in utter stillness.
But why does my heart sob in such anguish?

While stars sail in the celestial rivers,
subtle feelings and deep thoughts flow
through ethereal rills in my mind.

Snowy Village

Fresh, soft snow clothes
a small village in white:
Bare dormant trees,
roofs of thronged houses;
desolate lanes,
empty seashores;
And a lone wayfarer
on his winter journey.

Spring Storm

Chilly spring storms sweep
through desolate seashores.
Heavy, low clouds rush
in the gloomy night sky.

The moon peeks and hides
behind moving clouds.
Wild billows thunder
on the enraged sea.

My heaving spirit
soars up and plunges down,
in quick, vital rhythms
of Mother Nature.

Summer Sunset

Resplendent rays of the setting sun
glitter on the serene, mirror-like bay.

Shining pillars of the golden beams
arise from the calm sea to the azure sky.

At this moment of sheer splendours,
all things repose in deep sublimity.

Rumination

White autumnal frosts
shimmer on my hair.

My graceful flowers
of lush summers have fled
into our old, cherished
memories in my heart.

What I have sown in sweat,
I reap in thankfulness.

Sitting on thick piles
of colourful fallen leaves,
 I muse on this mysterious
 journey of my life.

Mute Songs

Leaving a faint track
on soft, fresh, deep snow,
I reach my open haven,
embraced by the sea.

Hungry creatures, bare trees,
frozen brooks—look, how
they wait for a new spring
in such stoical poises!

I kneel on the ground
to scribble in the snow
passionate yearnings
gushing from my heart.

Who would ever hear
these mute, secret songs,
echoing deeply within
a shy, lonesome heart?

Wandering Carefree

On a calm, sunny spring day
between dreary rainstorms,
I roam along vibrant seacoasts.

How wonderful to be free
from endless mundane cares!
I feel happy, like a bird
released from a stark cage.

Dews on a Rose

Fresh morning dews cling
to soft rose petals.
How pure and precious
they look like warm tears.

Why do you weep, my rose,
in such a subtle way?
Tell me the secrets
of your gentle heart.

{35}

Migrating Birds

Brilliant sunlight fills
the lucent autumn sky.
The vast sea reflects
resplendent lights and shades.

Flocks of migrating birds
fly aloft across the limpid sky.
How unearthly they look
like angels in the heavens!

A meek man prays
in heartfelt yearnings:
*"May you all come back home
safely in the new spring."*

On Freezing Seashores

Cold, arctic winds grip
this desolate land.
Massive ice prevails
wherever I look.

Misty, white vapours arise
from the freezing sea,
haunting like phantoms
in a strange daydream.

What am I seeking
on this stark seashore,
wandering all alone
in a sheer, waking dream?

Dismal Spring

Stormy, chilly rains drown
gloomy, bleak landscapes.

Dense fogs smother
all perspectives.

Dull days follow
one another endlessly.

My vague feelings fade
into dark oblivion.

Evening Stroll

On a balmy evening
after a sweet rainfall,
we stroll hand in hand
through Point Pleasant Park.

The setting sun pours out
resplendent golden rays,
gleaming on the calm bay
in glorious grandeur.

Cherished memories
of our youthful years
gush deep in our heart
like inner sunlight.

Autumn Woods

On the way to work,
I stop by the woods.
Leaves glow in bright hues.

Colourful leaves whisper
cherished memories
in their gentle rustles.

How much I wish to stay
longer in the deep woods,
sharing our joys and woes.

After the day's work,
I stop by the woods again.
Dusk shrouds us in dark veils.

Seasons' Flow

Stark frosts bedeck the frozen ground.
Dense fogs shroud desolate seashores.

A lone leaf trembles in the wind,
clinging to a frail, swaying branch.

A modest man bows to seasons' flow,
cherishing springs and summers past.

For Roses and Poems

I plant tender rosebushes
in our dormant garden,
dreaming of lush blossoms
of graceful, fragrant roses.

Tilling soil invigorates
my inert body to act.
Writing awakes my timid mind
to sing of sublime nature.

May pure, beautiful roses
and plain, honest poems
grow from warm sweat and tears
of my toil and love for them.

Gardening

Blissful summer days
bless an old gardener,
bowing modestly
to balmy, gentle breezes.

Beautiful roses bloom
in a splendid symphony
of vivid colours
and subtle fragrances.

Am I really awake
in my little garden?
Or do I waft afloat
in a midsummer's dream?

Touch of Autumn

The autumn deepens everywhere:
On misty shores of the serene sea;
In vivid, colourful, fallen leaves;
In the last rose of this season,
And in my inner reflection.

Winter Desolation

A lonely bird sits still
on frail, drifting ice.

How hungry it looks
amid this cold, harsh winter!

A man lingers alone
on this desolate shore.

What does he seek here
in such a forlorn mood?

Uneasy Spring

Bright sunshine glitters
in the sky, the land, and the sea.
A new timid spring sings
beneath melting snows.

Quick, playful waves dance
along vibrant seashores.
All creatures rejoice
at the mild breath of spring.

Yet, why do I feel
so numb and torpid?
A harsh winter lingers
in this uneasy heart.

Dawn

The picturesque bay is
imbued with the serene dawn.
All things seem to repose
in an ethereal dream.

These subtle lights and shades
before the calm sunrise
gently awake a meek soul
to breathe in the sublime.

Autumn Rose

A lonesome rose blooms
late in pensive autumn.
How ethereal it looks
in serene solitude!

Bees and butterflies
have gone with the lush summer.
For whom do you exude
such exquisite fragrances?

I kneel to breathe in
your blissful beauty.
May you ever bloom
deep in my warm heart.

Footprints on Snow

Fresh snow gently falls
on frozen seashores.

The calm sea reposes
in delicate mists.

A meek man strolls alone
rapt in deep thought.

A faint trace of footprints
fades in the sea of pure snow.

Spring Mists

Thin mists gently embrace
rugged, pristine seacoasts.

All things seem to dissolve
into subtle vapours.

Is this a magic spell
of the tender, balmy, new spring?

It enchants a meek man
to roam in a daydream.

Daydreaming

The glorious sun sets
beneath the horizon.
Subtle, warm afterglow
suffuses the mystic sea.

There must be someone
who admires this sunset,
looking at our world
from the other realm.

How much do I yearn
to see things unseen,
hidden afar beyond
my sight and insight.

Moonlit Garden

The bright autumn moon shines
on junipers and old driftwood
intertwining with green, mossy rocks.

Unearthly stillness deepens
 in this small private garden,
suffused by serene moonlight.

A shade of man sits still
rapt in deep meditation,
like a statue in an ancient temple.

Tides

Chilling winds gust through
desolate seashores.

The low tide exposes
strange rocks on the stark seabed.

A meek man stands still
on the bleak headland.

He muses on changing tides
in this mystic journey of our life.

Chilly Spring

Icebergs sail at sea.
Thick fogs engulf bleak seashores.
Dank, shy spring dithers.

Blessing

A young family plays
on a cozy, sheltered beach.

Gentle sea-breezes caress
lovely little children.

Wading carefree in lapping waves,
they collect exquisite seashells.

May the spiritual song of the sea
resound deeply ever in our hearts.

Toil and Prayer

I cover rosebushes
with thick fallen leaves,
cherishing the fragrances
of their graceful blooms.

I toil in tilling soil
to sow dormant seeds,
hoping that they will bear
good fruits in the following autumn.

I read immortal works
of my revered poets,
trying to breathe in deeply
their noble, lofty spirits.

I scribble on the bare ground
what I dream in earnest,
praying that they may bloom
into simple, pure songs.

A Wanderer

The ethereal bay gleams
in a serene, reflective sunset.

Soft afterglow suffuses
empty, tranquil seashores.

A worn-out seagull rests
on fragile, drifting ice.

A weary wanderer wonders
where he would find a home to rest.

Ode to Spring

I toil to till bare soils,
greeting a gentle new spring.
Tender, fresh buds sprout out
beneath the old, dead leaves.

How wondrous it is to see
the sheer drama of life,
unfolding its mystery
in such plain, usual ways.

We all have come from
the dust of past death,
and shall return to it
after our brief breath.

 May our fleeting sojourns
from the dust to the dust
bloom into timeless songs
from our hearts to our hearts.

A Heron

A graceful heron alights
on the pristine seashore
at a serene sunset
on a fine summer day.

It poises so still
like a mythical bird
in a sublime painting
of an unearthly world.

What does it ponder
in such a pensive mood?
Time seems to repose
in blissful peace.

Eloquent Autumn

The autumn deepens.

It paints everything
in subtle lights and shades.

Colourful leaves
gently fall off
from tall, old trees.

Fallen leaves bedeck
bleak, bare grounds
in exquisite patterns
of brilliant, primary hues.

How graciously they weave
rich, vivid memories
of lush, fervid summer
on their wide-open grave
in such an eloquent silence!

In a Waking Dream?

Long, hard work is done at last.
I walk home in a sea of snow.
The pale, weary sun sets in
drifting clouds over the frozen sea.

Subtle dusk embraces
my lone, empty shadow.
I pause to breathe in
this ethereal stillness.

Am I walking alone
in a waking dream,
humming homely hymns
to the mystic, inner realm?

Dao [道] is unseen, yet it inheres in everything.
Our life is brief, yet its spirit is timeless.

Epilogue

    This collection of simple songs
of our workaday life in flowing with
the natural cycles of seasons was gleaned
from my diaries over many years.

    I wish to thank my devoted wife,
Myonghae, who has sustained me to
endure and overcome struggles for
survival. Our beloved children—Grace,
Michael, David, and Florence— brought us
new tasks, goals, and hopes, which
inspired me to sing of our mundane life
with new meanings, zest, and devotion
in heartfelt thanks.

                                  Art Aeon

www.ingramcontent.com/pod-product-compliance
Lightning Source LLC
Chambersburg PA
CBHW031420040426
42444CB00005B/652